I Have Reaped Much More Than I Have Sown

My Career In Community Mental Health

Priscilla E. Pascual, M.S., LMFT

TABLE OF CONTENTS

DEDICATION

This is my tribute to the countless people: children, teens, adults, who have let me hear about their lives on my road to becoming a clinical therapist. Clients have taught me to sit with my values and honor them as my own, not to attribute them to others as if individuals should be like me. I have learned that I do not know what others need, as they are the ones who know what is missing from their lives or if their lives are simply fine as they are. As a therapist, I have learned that I cannot fix anything for anyone. It is a cruel reality that if something has been "broken" in life, there are real scars that can be with one forever.

ACKNOWLEDGMENTS

Thank you to my family: Claro, my husband and Jonathan and Reuben, our sons who have walked this path with me through school and career. There are always sacrifices that a spouse and children make when a parent engages in this type of pursuit. Patience, understanding and unconditional support have been given to me by them.

Thank you to Rachel Sugimoto, my sister who encouraged me in each step of my career and did the first edit of this work. Thank you also to Samuel Fillon, my brother, who took the time to review the first draft and offered feedback.

Thank you to Margaret Avineri, Psy. D., LMFT who set aside time to review this twice. I am grateful and so very appreciative of having these individuals in my life.

INTRODUCTION

My journey as a psychotherapist was one in which I took a step at a time, one hour at a time. I am recording that process here to encourage others who find themselves on an arduous road wondering where it will take them and asking as children often do, "Are we there yet?" As I began this chapter later in life, I did so with the wisdom that, in theory, I knew what I was going after, but with the blissful ignorance of not knowing what a challenge it was to get there. This book also tells the stories of clients whose names are fictional, but the stories are real.

As I am retiring from the formal part of my career, speaking with my most recent manager, I told her that on reflection, I have never grieved the stories of these individuals. As a therapist, when we sit with someone telling us of their deepest pain, we are trained to be able to "contain" their feelings, hold that "space" for them as they grieve right in front of us. We do not burst into tears as we do not want clients to have to comfort us. We still feel like bursting into tears because we are human. I have been stunned into silence by things I have heard and have sat with those I have supervised when they have begun crying during supervision with me about a client's terrible experience of abuse.

In writing this, it is a time that I can work through my own tears because of the sadness, the hopelessness, and the devastating trauma folks experience daily. I also want to celebrate the victories and the amazing resiliency of people who carry on after suffering things beyond what a human should have to endure.

CHAPTER ONE

THE JOURNEY BEGINS

My first exposure to the world of therapy came as a secretary in a child psychiatry clinic at a county hospital. Although I know my father was disappointed that I did not go to college upon graduation from high school, he was always an encourager and said, "Be the best secretary you can be!" He said, "All work is honorable." I was the secretary to the head physician, a child psychiatrist who was the clinical supervisor for residents who would rotate through our program to satisfy the requirements to become psychiatrists.

In child psychiatry, I worked with psychologists and social workers. Observing them, I was drawn to the social workers, and I know that they influenced me in my eventual choice to be like them. I mentioned this to another secretary whom I used to supervise, and she frankly said to me, "I do not know how you could be a social worker. You have no compassion!" Well, wow. I guess asking her to do her job translated into a lack of compassion. I never took to heart what she said, as I knew very much who I was, and I was not a person who lacked compassion. I have always been direct, however, and perhaps it was my style of communication that needed a little work.

Several years later, I was married and the mother of two boys, and I began thinking of going to college. My two sons are five years apart, and so when the second one entered kindergarten, I found myself driving down the street alone for the first time in ten years with two hours to spend each day all by myself.

I spoke with my husband and let him know I wanted to take a class during those two hours and that "if I don't learn something every day, I will quit!" I recall saying those words, and now decades later find that every day brings something new if you really care to see and learn.

I enrolled at the local junior college with no timeline, as I was not there to prove anything or do something I had missed. I was there to work around the lives of my children and husband and attend a class.

Political Science was my first class, which for me was an odd choice, but it fit into my busy mom's schedule. I was in for a surprise as I met a gifted instructor who challenged me in this area of learning. As I finished his class, I chose another and with my second son staying in school longer, I was able to take two classes. Before I knew it, I had accumulated enough units to transfer to the local university to further my exploration of higher education. Still, I had no career path in mind, and I just followed the college catalogue to make sure I got a degree in something.

At some point, when I was speaking with my sister, Rachel, she mentioned to me a career in counseling. She was in therapy herself and all I knew about therapy was really from her. I thought about it more and knew that this would be helpful to me as I served in our local church as a Sunday school teacher. After earning my degree in sociology with a minor in psychology, I applied to the Marriage, Family and Child Counseling program at the university. After the requisite interviews, I was accepted and then began, in earnest, my path toward a master's degree.

There are many ways to do therapy, countless theories, and approaches. This is what I have learned through my education and experience—it is not meant to be an exhaustive study on the therapeutic process as I am limited, of course, and am still growing and developing. I am simply sharing my journey in this helping profession and the rewarding relationships I have had along the way.

CHAPTER TWO

COUNSELING/PSYCHOLOGY IN THE 1990S

I never thought about how exclusive psychotherapy was in the 1990s. It was expensive to be in therapy, and I never met a therapist in the circle of people I knew. I was focused on becoming a therapist and did not consider how out of place this might be for a person such as myself.

As an ethic minority growing up, I knew I was different than my peers, and I just dealt with it. In the city where I was raised, there was a sprinkling of Latinos and Asians and no African Americans. All the children were trying to fit in, but there was a distinct difference between those minorities who were of a lower-socioeconomic group. Those Latinos who were a bit higher in the order of things were not always so kind to me. In fact, I was discriminated against more by them than by other groups.

Because my father was a Filipino immigrant and my mother was a Texas Mexican, I grew up in a multicultural environment. I was not "Filipino" enough for my Filipino relatives and did not feel "Mexican" enough when with Mexican cousins who were all bi-lingual. It was a challenge for me when my cousins could speak fluently with my mono-lingual Spanish-speaking grandmother, and I would be standing there wishing I could join in the conversation, feeling left out.

Throughout my life, people assumed I was Spanish speaking and when meeting Filipinos, they asked why I did not speak their language. The answer is simple. My father spoke Ilocano, a Filipino dialect and my mother spoke Spanish. Both used their native tongue throughout their lives, but in our home, we spoke English as that was the common language of us all.

Entering the counseling/therapist world, all was new to me. Reality quickly set in, as during my first semester in graduate school I had to find an agency where I could see clients to gain therapy hours. The freeways in Southern California and surrounding areas take you anywhere you would like to go. The 405, the 110 going north and south, with the 91 and the 105 intersecting and taking you east and west. The first half of my career as a therapist found me on the 405 each day traveling toward the beach to spend my time working at a non-profit community counseling center. This was my first placement, beginning the journey toward licensure.

There were few paid traineeships, so I worked for the joy of it. When I became an intern, I treated children in a school program, making $10.00 an hour. During that time, a little client of mine said during our session, "YOU get PAID for this?" I thought, "not enough to be seeing you, honey." You could say this child was "difficult to sit with." But, "Yes" I got paid.

At this agency, I learned the basics of the therapeutic process, having skilled supervisors who came alongside to help lead me in my journey as a mental health clinician. I was working on my hours required by the State of California (seeing clients, learning the paperwork, and the legal and ethical guidelines that are needed with this license). I was sitting under amazing supervisors each week wondering when I would ever be like them. In the process, I learned to do therapy.

Growing into my Licensed Marriage and Family Therapist shoes was a formidable and incredibly arduous task. Each hour of the three thousand must be supervised, and therefore, all through my training I had individual and group supervision by licensed therapists. I was supervised by LMFTs (Licensed Marriage and Family Therapist), Psy. Ds (Doctor of Psychology), Ph.Ds. (Doctor of Philosophy), and LCSWs (Licensed Clinical Social Worker.)

During weekly supervision we would present our cases, receiving guidance and feedback on what happened "in the room" with clients we were seeing. Our supervisors would hear what sounded like ramblings at times as to what happened that week. It was often hard to frame into a simple statement or question where we were "stuck" or where we needed help. Forget being too proud to ask the question. In group supervision, I was usually there with six or seven individuals for two hours and eventually my supervisor would mercilessly get around to me. Or so it felt with Dahlia.

Reflecting on my first supervisor, Dahlia, when I began my traineeship, I can well imagine her thinking, "One of These Things (Is Not Like the Others)" (Raposo, 1968) a song on a children's program which I would watch with my sons. Being a Filipino-Mexican, I was a standout, in addition to the fact that I was about 20 years older than everyone else. It seemed, at times, that Dahlia did not like me as her responses often sounded hostile and impatient. More about Dahlia later.

In the counseling community, I found myself at workshops and dinners for therapists in the area as I belonged to the requisite organizations for counselors. These social gatherings were stressful as I found myself looking for someone with whom to sit, like the lunch tables in elementary school. Along with my husband who is Filipino, we were the only ethnically different people usually present, except for the wait staff. I discovered my peers were not the friendliest, which is interesting because therapists should be engaging and welcoming. My husband and I ended up speaking with each other while at these events. We were at a loss as to how to jump in on a conversation with a group of therapists who were sharing their recent travels abroad, upcoming conferences they were going to attend, and their spouse's project of restoring their vintage car. Therapists would be networking with each other, as they were in private practice, and since I was in non-profit, this was not something I ever did. There appeared to be a class difference.

There are class differences in all areas of life, but it was noticeably clear to me through my years working near the beach. My zip code was different than the others. My peers had beach city addresses or were from "the hill" the beautiful peninsula overlooking the Pacific Ocean. Those I supervised were children of high-powered attorneys and doctors all raised in affluent communities. That was okay. I had wonderful relationships with many and forged friendships that remained throughout my career.

CHAPTER THREE

SUPERVISION, SUPERVISORS, SUPERVISING

Dahlia, my first supervisor, was the epitome of someone living and working in an exclusive area. She was slender, dressed in casual chic. She practiced using psychodynamic theory. She was an intimidating supervisor, and I was afraid to say anything. My colleagues (one was a graduate of the Naval Academy and at that time an engineer) felt the same way. Everything we said was wrong, or so it seemed. She looked at us disapprovingly with each word we spoke as if we were ignorant children.

As I mentioned previously, Dahlia had a disdain for me. Although I did not fit in with the look of a "budding therapist" my colleagues were good people, treated me well, all "trainees" who knew about as much as I did, which was nothing. There was an exception, Annabelle, who was married to an actor and used a treatment modality which included dream interpretation. Impressive.

One day a colleague from the group, Linda, told me, "She seems harder on you." It was not my imagination. One time I was speaking about a case, Dahlia interrupted me and said, "Is there a question in there somewhere?" Another time, my very first client came and announced that she was ending treatment because she found a therapist who took her insurance. I reviewed what we had covered together and wished her well. When I shared this with my supervision group Dahlia said, "Therapy is messy, and you tried to tie it up with a nice little bow?" I was speechless as this was my first client, my first termination, and I just did what anyone would do, ending a brief relationship abruptly. I did the best I could. Dahlia would do this to me and others, but because the time of her group fit with my busy school/mom schedule, I just plugged along.

During my time with Dahlia a friend came into supervision and was thrilled because she had a good session and was eager to share. After Daisy enthusiastically spoke about the wonders of the session, our supervisor said, "What makes you think that was a good session?" Daisy was crushed and humiliated as she struggled to respond. Daisy never returned and left her counseling career entirely.

For the rest of us, it just confirmed what we already knew, that our supervisor had "issues" and that we were sitting in an emotionally hostile environment. After Daisy left the agency, the agency directors called me to let me know I could leave Dahlia's group if I wished. They asked me what it was about the supervisor that was so off-putting and scary. I responded, "Her presentation. She is very reactive."

I decided to tough it out with Dahlia, as I said. It was fun to sit with someone from the Naval Academy who was also scared of her and experience another colleague who would only look at me whenever he presented a case. He never looked at our supervisor when he spoke; he looked at me. It was an awkward mess. I remember another friend would wear patterned sweaters to group and I would sit there looking at the patterns trying to figure them out. I was disassociating.

It is astounding to me that Dahlia never processed what our group was feeling/experiencing while in our two-hour meetings.

Talk about "the elephant in the room." We resembled the dynamics of a dysfunctional family at Thanksgiving dinner, with us at the "children's table." And so, it went on for an entire year.

My second supervisor, Eva, was working from a "family systems" perspective. She was so highly intelligent, and I was just in awe of the questions she would ask to assess a client. She would supply amazing feedback in just a few sentences, and I always thought, "How did she do that?" She conceptualized cases so easily. Through the years since, I would ask myself, "How did this client get from 'there' (in the womb), to 'here' sitting in front of me now?" I credit Eva with my own conceptualization skill which I feel is one of my strengths. Eva is the one who instilled in me that I was in the right field. She knew me better than I knew myself— and she believed in me until I believed in myself as a therapist.

My third supervisor was Faith. It was from Faith that I learned empathy "putting yourself in someone's shoes" is something that a therapist must continually do to gain perspective on a case. When you have empathy for someone, you are not feeling sorry for them. It is going from "That is a sad story," to a clearer understanding of how that sad story came to be and a better grasp of how your client felt while having to walk that path.

Faith was very gentle, and everyone wanted to be supervised by her. She is the one who taught me to name things as they are so that I am understood, and the hearer is clear on what we are talking about. As an example, I had an adult client who was particularly challenging to me, and he even scared me a bit as he was explosive. In supervision I said, "and I told him that we would get through this together." Faith followed up with, "What is 'this?' What were you talking about?" The answer was, "His ritualized sexual abuse at the hands of school staff when he was in preschool." The topic was too difficult for me at that time to digest and so I just walked around it. If I, as a therapist, was too scared to speak about the reality of a situation, how could I help my wounded client work through what happened to him?

Therefore, I want to make sure that my supervisees truly hear what I am saying. I tell them, "Our work is too important to be wondering about what we are discussing." Or, I have said, "Are we on the same page?" If the answer is "Yes" then the follow-up from me would be, "What page is that?" and have them repeat what our plan going forward is to be.

Faith and Eva were great colleagues. They were strong, intelligent individuals, both Doctors of Psychology, who poured themselves into me. Faith was the one who interviewed me for the placement and said that I had valuable life experience which would help me in this profession. Faith died years later. What a tremendous loss to the counseling community, to her supervisees who loved being in her presence, and to the world which was graced with her lovely and gentle ways.

Charles was one of our clinical directors. He received his Ph.D. from a prestigious university and told us all—if you need a doctorate, just get it anyway you can, referring to how difficult a process this was. He was from the southern part of the United States and spoke with a drawl. He was beyond thoughtful and took his time to answer any comment or question. Since he was the clinical director, we waited for what seemed like forever for him to speak.

As a therapist, I used to feel compelled to respond quickly to a client because silence would make me feel uncomfortable. A therapist does not have the answer to everything, and I have learned to acknowledge the difficult question and to say, "I do not know. I will have to think about that one." Or I have said, "Let's sit here and see what we come up with," supporting the client in the moment to discover the answer to the question themself.

I have learned that as a supervisor, the setting must always be non-threatening, non-judgmental, welcoming, and safe. Supervision is where a therapist reveals who they are, how they think, always looking inward to see how they can grow personally and professionally. Supervisors are not there to tell a supervisee what to do. They are there as guides so that the supervisee can learn that there are many ways to function in a therapeutic setting. As each client and therapist is unique, it is the therapist's job to challenge themself to figure out how that is done, as each client needs the best approach suited for them.

I always knew I wanted to become a clinical supervisor. I loved to supervise. I was surrounded by bright individuals who were working toward psychology, social work, marriage, family, and child therapy degrees. They were enthusiastic about developing skills to hopefully help children and their families to have better relationships, more understanding, healing of emotional wounds and encouraging souls in a sometimes-heartless world.

I have found that most master's level individuals are "A" students. They sit in the front row in school and excel trying to be the best they can. When someone sits in their first supervision, speaking about real people who are depending upon them to help them in their lives through therapy, it is very humbling to realize how little one knows about how this is done. A brand-new therapist must sit in front of the scrutinizing eye of their supervisor, trying to figure out how to form a question without sounding stupid. I can of course, speak only for myself. Individuals are vulnerable going through this process. Humility comes in handy.

When I meet a supervisee for the first time, keeping in mind the requirements for their position, I ask myself two questions. The first is "What do I need from this supervisee?" The second is "What do they need from me so that I can help support them in meeting their goals?"

I have supervised interns, associates (those who have graduated with their master's degree), and those who are licensed, such as LMFTs LCSWs and Psy.Ds. The way I supervise has been influenced by those who supervised me, which is natural. I also learned from inadequate supervisors. (Yes, the therapist knows when they are sitting with someone who knows less than they do, or at least I did).

Supervision is a mutually respectful relationship. I should have respect from the supervisee, and I am respectful of them. I respect the difficulty all who have gone through to get to the place that they are in that moment.

I respect their histories, as we all have one which has shaped our view of the world and has contributed to our choice of becoming a therapist. Individuals have been wounded in their life and this can help or interfere in the way they work with others.

I need to put a clinician in context. I ask why they have chosen counseling, why they are working with this population of clients, and I ask them to tell me about their family. I do not need details. I just need a framework from which they and I can grow together. I want to have the "whole person" sitting in front of me as the "whole person" needs to grow and develop.

Supervision is not therapy. Many clinicians are in their own therapy or seek support as they need it during their career. If a supervisee is constantly bringing their own baggage into the room, their supervisor must address it as it may influence their work with the clients the supervisee treats.

As an illustration a co-facilitator of mine and I were leading a parenting group. At times, she would become so immersed in the story of one of the parents and begin to do individual therapy with them in the middle of the session. I followed up with her and said, "I notice that when you are hearing the client's story, you become that client –everyone is you." I recommended that she go to therapy herself to work on her incredibly challenging past.

As another example, a supervisee of mine hated tattoos. I had no idea that tattoos triggered her until one of her teen clients got one. The therapist came to supervision and angrily expressed to me how she told this young girl about all the negatives of getting a tattoo. After the therapist's rant I said, "You sound just like a parent. As a therapist, is there another way you could have approached this? What do you think?"

I see my supervisees. I see their strengths, support them when they need a boost, and reach out to them if they are drowning. (I recall trying to learn to swim and how I knew I would never master this skill. I was the exception to the law that humans can swim. I was special. I tried in pools, in the ocean and always had someone say, "You are doing it! You are swimming!" I would think, "No, I am drowning so please do not call 'drowning' 'swimming' as I may look like I can do this, but I cannot.") It is a terrible feeling when one knows that they are overwhelmed and on the brink of failing, and others are oblivious and tell them that they are doing fine when they are not.

For example, I have had individuals behind and confused with the paperwork, the timelines, and other requirements of their position. I have had to ask, "Can you do this job?" I had one say, "I think I can, do you?" I responded, "I don't know." Then followed the conversation of what I was seeing in them and asking them to tell me where they were struggling so that we could plan together for success.

I am transparent and authentic. As I have worked in organizations that are non-profit, I do not hide things from my team members about what may be coming down the proverbial company pipe. I transition to hard topics over time, as it is allowable. I gently let them know a new requirement is coming around the corner and how I am there to support if it is overwhelming and challenging.

I also let people know that no one I know has ever been fired for doing their absolute best. When an individual has put it out there and has worked their hardest, has pulled from every resource and still not made the grade, then perhaps the position is not for them.

In graduate school, we had a culminating, written examination, called The Comps. We had two readers/ reviewers of our exam with whom we would meet to go over the exam orally. The tests were different, and I was hoping for one that did not have a question on substance abuse. Of course, sitting down for the test, there it was. I remember looking at another student in the exam room at that moment as we had discussed beforehand hoping a question on this subject was not there. Our eyes locked, the look of "Oh well" came over our faces as we began.

After the exam, we were told who our two readers or professors were. Fortunately, one was Dr. Johnstone, who was brilliant and an amazing clinician. Unfortunately, the other was Dr. Smythe, who was known for her critical and punishing ways. When my appointment arrived, I went to Dr. Smythe's office where she was sitting behind her desk and my other professor was off to the side leaning up against another desk in the room. He clearly did not think that this would take long, as he did not even sit.

As we reviewed the test, we came to the substance abuse question, my kryptonite. I tried to answer the question and when I finished, Dr. Smythe asked for "more." Well, she repeated this two times. All the while, Dr. Johnstone was getting increasingly annoyed with Dr. Smythe for her overkill on this one question. After she asked for the third time, I said "This is all I have. I have nothing more to add." At that point, Dr. Johnstone looked at Dr. Smythe and said, "Pass?" with his arms extended and his palms up in a pleading manner as he wanted this unnecessary torturous moment to end. Dr. Smythe did not say "pass." She said, "You won't get away with this at the state orals, Priscilla!" as I gathered my wits and my backpack and left the room. State exam? I thought, "Am I there already? Aren't there years to go yet? Thanks, Dr. Smythe for caring so far in advance." I think she hated me.

After that experience, I realized that when there is nothing left and you have given all you have to give, just say it. "Got nothing." Because I did not. And if my answers were not as magnificent as she hoped they would be, "So be it." I have followed that principle since then. I work hard up front, always do my part, exceed expectations, and if that is not enough, then that is okay. In the end, the one who must be satisfied with my performance is me. Period.

I remember how I felt as a trainee, as an intern and every step I had to take to get my license. I will never forget where I have come from, as a therapist is forever a work in progress.

Working in a non-profit as a supervisor, our clients came in and were assigned to clinicians who had openings. This is one reason I had to know who my supervisees were. Knowing their strengths and their challenges, I could match them as closely as possible with clients with whom they could work successfully.

Because our cases were all trauma cases, as I mentioned previously, a clinician's history came into play continually. A therapist's history would show itself in many ways, including overidentifying with the client, frustration, anger, and impatience if the client were not progressing quickly enough according to the therapist.

A case came across my desk which was one of a teen client just coming out as gay. The first thought was to assign the client to a gay therapist whom I supervised. This was an obvious match, however I wanted to know if this client wanted a gay therapist or if they would feel patronized if we assigned a gay clinician because the client was gay.

I am using this as an example as when someone comes to therapy, it is a huge decision. It is important that we not assume from the beginning assessment that we know what someone wants. We must ask.

Another teen client came in who needed to process a rape, the resultant pregnancy, and her parents forcing her to have an abortion. The young girl's case was given to a clinician who began seeing her, but soon after found out that she herself was pregnant.

It was obvious that this therapeutic relationship could not continue. We developed a careful plan so that the client would understand why after the therapeutic relationship had already been established, it had to end. This was another loss for the client as the reassignment was carried out.

As a supervisor, it was my job to bring up topics with the clinician as they pertained to the work with a client. One therapist had a client who was overweight, who had come in with this as a primary issue. Her therapist was also struggling with her weight. During the time they worked together, the therapist began a program to lose her extra pounds and her weight loss began to show. The client's weight remained the same. The topic of conversation with the therapist was how to manage questions if there were any, about her own weight loss and process the feelings of the client because she was still significantly overweight.

Any change in the composition of the relationship should be addressed by the therapist if the client brings it up. If the therapist comes into session wearing an engagement ring, or a wedding ring not previously worn, there are boundaries that would be observed by the therapist. The therapist is opening a door, however, which they need to be prepared to address. As a pregnant therapist begins to "show" the pregnancy tells the client a lot about a therapist that may not have been previously disclosed. How these situations are managed would be at the discretion of the therapist.

Working in a non-profit company we see clients who are desperately poor, often ignored and of course, deeply wounded. We were in the community doing home visits and one never knew what the situation might be upon arrival at a home. Awareness of boundaries must always be in place, and it is the clinician's duty to make sure they are held. Clients who have been violated are vulnerable and may have poor boundaries, so a clinician should not expect a client to set limits.

One of my team members was a tremendously empathetic therapist who was the grandpa every child would want to have. He always wore a suit and necktie, drove a new car and was gentle and kind. His clients and their siblings loved to see him when he arrived at their home.

We had discussions about how families viewed him and how they may have wished he were their grandfather. I remember that after a certain case was closed, he received a call from the family. They wanted him to attend the birthday celebration of his former client. Of course, he could not attend as therapists are not supposed to have a personal association with former clients until after a period of years and even then, it must be evaluated closely for appropriateness. When he received the call, however, he was caught off guard and so he simply told them he had a conflict in his schedule.

When he told me about the phone call, we reviewed why he could not go: his relationship with the client was a professional one and not a friendship. If he attended, boundaries could be blurred, and it would be defined as a "dual relationship" which is unethical. These discussions with clients are sensitive and clients may get their feelings hurt in the process. Conversations about this should be held at the beginning of therapy so that clients understand the role of the therapist as it can easily be misinterpreted.

Often clients prepare food for therapists. Dinner may be on the stove when the therapist arrives. One such time a therapist was caught in a quandary when she was offered food and she was aware that the family's resources were limited. Cultural issues were present, and the therapist had to decide what to do so that she did not insult the client's mother by refusing the food.

Another clinician noticed that the mother of the client would bake something special for him when he arrived for therapy with her child. He had to address the situation as it became a clinical issue. He clarified that the purpose of the visits was for the mental health of her child and as kind as it was for her to prepare something to eat, he asked her to stop as the relationship was a professional one.

One client told me at the end of the session that she would come to see me, tell me about her life in detail but that she did not know anything about me. I responded that this was true. We then explored how this type of relationship felt for her, that it was different and not a friendship, and what that meant. We spoke about what she would prefer it to be like and how that would impact what she shared with me. Acknowledging that the relationship was therapeutic and at times complicated, we agreed that she was there for herself. She was not there to learn about me.

As therapists, we want to model authentic and honest conversations. As difficult as it may be to have these types of communications with individuals, if it can be done it will explain the relationship as to what it really means to each one as they work together.

A supervisor will have challenging feedback to offer to supervisees. I have explained that as therapists, we are assessing people all the time, and we need to be able to be looked at by others. We assess and are in turn assessed. Through the years, I have learned to ask for feedback at the end of each supervision. I have also practiced giving positive feedback to my supervisees on things I have noticed during the hour, and to comment also on areas needing growth. I have had uncomfortable moments and I am sure they have had some as well. It is important that a good rapport has been established as it can sustain these moments. They can help both supervisor and supervisee grow and develop.

Ethics and law are a vital part of being a good therapist. I have appreciated working at agencies because of the oversight and guidelines that must be followed. When individuals work on their own, as in private practice, it is incumbent upon them to follow the laws and ethics of our profession. It can be done of course, but keeping good boundaries and working for the good of the client may sometimes get muddled. In private practice there may be isolation without checks and balances. Meeting with other therapists, discussing issues of concern, and consulting with good mentors are all ways to support a therapist and provide self-care.

Chapter Four

Clients

In my first setting, because of my age I was assigned middle-aged women. They had figuratively "hit the wall" as they finally noticed it was their looks that kept them afloat in life and that when the first wrinkles appeared, their worth diminished. I realize that is simplistic, however through the years, I have seen how important it is to know who you are on the inside, rather than from what people see.

Life changes people and life can be cruel. If we are dependent upon others to affirm us without first affirming ourselves, we will soon find out that the validating confirmations from others fade over time. The trappings we relied upon for so long are haggard and worn or just gone.

When I received my first assignment, the client's fee to the agency was $40.00 per session. I could only think that it was a rip-off as my self-worth as a therapist was lacking. I could not believe that someone would pay to sit with me for 50 minutes. I told my clinical director that I needed to go home to process the fact that someone else's mental health was in what I thought were my unqualified hands, which was true. I needed a nap.

Another early-on client came in and she was a runner, complete with attire showing her toned body. Although I had jogged for years for exercise in what seemed like another life, I told Charles, "My running shoes are bronzed and on my coffee table," wondering how I would be able to connect with this individual since we were from such different worlds. His advice was, "Just go in there and do your best 'Carl Rogers.'" (Rogers, 1961). I have used this advice and have passed it on to countless supervisees throughout the years.

While it is great to be able to be a perfect match between therapist and client, I have worked cross-culturally throughout my entire career. Cross culture is usually thought of in terms of race and ethnicity, however it also refers to age, gender, sexual orientation, religion, etc., as well. Therefore, it is good practice to address these differences with the client as someone in their twenties, for example, can be assigned to work with much older clients, such as grandparents or seniors.

Years ago, I was at a wedding and sitting with a woman about 55 years old. As we conversed, we spoke about my being a therapist, as the bride, our mutual friend was a therapist as well. This individual said that she was a client at the clinic where I worked. She went on to say that she was in the waiting room for her first session and, "In walked a boy." She mentioned his name and I knew him, a twenty-something who was an exceptionally good clinician. She said she had misjudged him at first sight, as he was the best therapist she ever had.

A new supervisee of mine went out on a case in which the primary caregiver was a grandmother. She had already raised her own children and now, single-handedly, was raising her grandchildren. The new therapist came back from her first appointment frustrated, and exclaimed, "I can't tell her anything!" I responded, "No you cannot." This weary grandmother had been parenting for decades and this young individual with two degrees was not able to tell her about a "better way" to parent her grandson referred by the school because of misbehavior.

So now what? Well, one begins with humility by thanking the grandmother for allowing the therapist into her home. The grandmother is the "expert" as this is her household. The therapist will genuinely acknowledge the grandmother's efforts and let her know that the therapist is there for support. The therapist can ask what she needs to assist her to help make raising the children a bit easier. As we were a non-profit our therapists also did case management. Families need food, clothing etc., and while there are social service agencies that provide these things, our agency also linked clients to assistance.

I have had bridges to build throughout the years collaborating with clients, peers, and team members from different demographics. I have never had an issue come up of not being able to work with an individual because of differences. Being older in my case helped as I knew who I was as a person, dealt with discrimination my whole life and knew where that belonged in my overall experience.

I believe that in this career, we can work successfully because we all share similarities. We are human. We have experienced joy, sadness, and trauma. We have bled, laughed, and cried, and been on the brink of giving up. Success has just been "around the corner" and failure followed closely behind. We have been embarrassed and humiliated. We are human and therein lies the connection. Our humanity.

Dana. Dahlia was my supervisor when I began treating Dana, who threatened suicide every time the sun did not shine. "It's a great day for it today," she would say, looking out the window. And as I thought, "Here we go again" I began to assess her plan, intent, and means. During the winter, we went through this quite a lot and I asked my supervisor, "Do I have to assess every time she says it?" The answer was "Yes." So, I did. Week after week.

I was still working with Dana when I transitioned to Eva, and I presented my case. Eva listened to Dana's history and noted that Dana had been in therapy for an exceedingly long time. Eva said in effect that I would have to find another way to treat this client. What? What is another way? I did not even know the first way at that point. Where do I look? Can someone give me a clue?

This was when I had to learn how to use "the relationship." Although I had seven supervisors who trained me, Faith and Eva were outstanding. As much as I learned from them, the most important principle of being a therapist was that "the relationship" between the clinician and the client was vital. No relationship, no trust, no safety. No relationship, no techniques or interventions need to be brought into the mix. No relationship, no healing. No relationship, time wasted. I still believe this. It is paramount in how I work as a therapist and as a supervisor.

There was not a whole lot of movement in treatment, as far as I could see. Dana just told me of her life. I sat and listened, reflected, and built a relationship with Dana which lasted over a year. She was a lonely individual who never fit in and had to hide who she was, except from me.

Dana was severely physically abused by her mother. She would sleep at night with her arms across her body to protect herself from her mother who would beat her with clothes hangers or any other device nearby. This abuse was from early on. Once I asked Dana how far back, she could remember it happening, and she said, "the crib." That is what she said. As a therapist, we do not investigate what our clients tell us for its truthfulness unless of course, it is a case where you are challenging irrational thinking or if you are working with someone whose goal may be to increase being truthful.

There is research on how much an adult can remember from their childhood experiences, but for the purpose of sharing Dana's truth, we can suspect that she was physically and emotionally abused by her mother for as long as she could recall. There was no secure attachment in her life. She never felt safe as no one cared for her. She had built a fortress around herself, rarely betraying feelings as they were too painful to acknowledge and to express.

Dana came from a wealthy family, which presented a beautiful picture to the world. Inside was pain and suffering for Dana. Dana told me that she would go to her grandmother's home nearby where she sought refuge. Her grandmother would send her back home with "I'll pray for you." As well-meaning as her grandmother was, she was part of a closed family system that took care of business within the family and whose dirty laundry was never seen by anyone but the housekeeper.

Dana had been in longstanding lesbian relationships. I had the opportunity to meet her then-partner, Jenny, as the day came when Dana needed to be hospitalized. I asked Dana to come into the office with Jenny. My director, Charles met with Dana and myself and let her know that after speaking with me, it was necessary for us to have Dana volunteer for hospitalization to keep her safe. She was cooperative in response to my director, who amazed me with his calm and gentle presence as we spoke of going to the hospital. His tone and manner were as normal as asking if we wanted to go to get some ice cream from the nearby shop. He was that non-threatening and so exceedingly kind. I, on the other hand, had no experience with a suicidal client, and I was trying to calm myself so that I would be of some use to Dana.

As he was assessing, he joined with Dana as he told a story of how he felt hopeless and desperate when his fiancée broke off their engagement. At this point, I almost fell off my non-profit sofa! What? He was disclosing information about himself. I had learned in counseling 101 that you never tell the client anything about yourself. Charles was violating the rules. Since then, I have discovered things about appropriate disclosure. He was not using it to ask Dana to take care of him or feel sorry for him; he was using it to let her know he understood her pain. He acknowledged that, yes, life is so difficult that at times one may feel that the only answer is suicide.

As we drove to the hospital, I was anxious and uncertain as I had never done this before, and it was more than daunting. At the hospital we took the elevator to the top floor, and we entered a hell hole of a psychiatric unit, right out of horror movies. There was a stench of body odor. The walls needed painting, and a patient was lying on a bed half naked with the door open. I thought, "Oh my, this is a nightmare. Now what?"

It was then that Dana spoke up and said, "I am not staying here; it is not safe. Look over there. I can hang myself with that," pointing to an electrical cord on the floor. Yep. About that time, the director of the unit came over to greet us as if he were representing the executive suites at a five-star hotel downtown. I thought, "Is he for real? Does he not see what we see?" As Dana was standing right by me and I was the therapist, I summoned my courage and said to him, "My client does not feel safe here. We will not be staying." His face changed and he understood completely. Up until that moment, he had a role to play.

He then went to the telephone to make a call to check if there was an opening across town at another psychiatric facility. I called

my director at our agency to let him know that our plans changed
and why. Soon we went on our way to the second hospital.
Thankfully, this hospital was clean, welcoming, and secure. Dana
agreed to stay for what ended up being three weeks. She tried to
kill herself while hospitalized but was stabilized by the doctors and
released to outpatient care once again.

When she came back for her first appointment after being
discharged, our clinical director met with us and apologized
profusely for sending us to the first hospital. Dana responded
amazingly to him, and I guess would have loved to continue as his
client if she could, as Charles was the consummate clinician.

My direct supervisor, Eva told me that what saved Dana from
killing herself right before she was hospitalized, was the
relationship she had with me. She was confident of that. Although
I cannot take credit for Dana's living, I began to realize the
powerfulness of connection, of relationship, unconditionally.
Being myself with this client, listening, deeply caring for her, total
acceptance despite our differences, being able to sit with her in an
authentic way because of our similarities, was healing.

After about another year, Dana decided to go back home, out
of state, and we had to say farewell. She asked to see a picture of
my family so that she could put me in context. In our last session, I
brought in a photo of myself with my husband and two sons. She
smiled broadly and thanked me for doing that for her. Dana is the
only one who asked to see my family and she is the only one in 30
years with whom I have shared their picture. I do not know exactly
what that meant to her, but it appeared to mean a lot. The last time
I heard from her was through a postcard that simply said, "Know
this, I am alive because of you." I wonder about her often and am
so glad that I was a part of Dana's life.

Olivia. Olivia was in treatment for depression and anxiety. She was an executive at a company, and she often had anxious moments when she led meetings. She referred to her mother as cold and unfeeling, like "ice." Olivia was estranged from her mother, and her father had died years before.

Working to reduce her anxiety, I remember doing visualization with her and in one session as we began, I closed my eyes and made sure she was comfortable closing hers as well. I started speaking in a soft and soothing voice, describing a picture of pleasant surroundings, trickling brook included. At one point, I opened my eyes and there was Olivia peeking at me with a smile on her face. So, when we both burst into laughter I thought, "Okay, so that did not work. Let us just talk."

In class one evening at school, we discussed Gestalt (Perl's, F., Hefferline R., Goodman, P, 1951) and his use of the "empty chair." The intervention *du jour* for Olivia that next session was exactly that. Olivia had unfinished business with her deceased father and so we set up the intervention by visualizing her dad in the chair. As Olivia began to speak, she became increasingly agitated and started screaming at her "dad" in the chair. While this would be perfectly fine, the treatment room was adjacent to the waiting room, which had paper-thin walls. I began to feel panicky because she was not stopping, and instead she was escalating. I just sat there quietly, praying for a "divine" intervention. I was not prepared for what I was experiencing and was wondering how I was supposed to contain my client and her explosive emotions in that moment.

I mentioned this in group supervision with Dahlia. For the life of me, given the fact that in Dahlia's eyes I already seemed without therapeutic skills, I wonder why I risked bringing it to supervision only to be humiliated once again. In retrospect, I just really wanted to learn. As she was psychodynamic in preference of treatment, she scoffed at other therapeutic approaches. After I presented my experience she said, "When did you realize that you had lost control of the session?" I was speechless, of course, because Olivia did calm down (after what seemed like an eternity), and we were both safe and she left the session all in one piece!

Dahlia continued, "For those of you who prefer to work this way…" I was not preferring anything; just trying to figure out how therapy worked. I was still in school and learning as I went. Anyway, I forgot the full lecture from that point on, as I was thinking about how many hours I had to go before I reached three thousand. What is three thousand minus nineteen hours? Hmmm, this is going to be an awfully long period of my life.

Next session with Olivia, she commented on the empty chair (Perls, 1951) and told me she had turned a corner with her dad. It had helped her tremendously and she said she almost contacted me mid-week to let me know. Although it was a positive result, after that I left the Gestalt interventions to those who knew what they were doing.

Cynthia. Cynthia was one of the best bartenders at a topless bar in town where folks would come just to watch her tend bar. She was a raspy voiced, petite blond-haired woman who was a courageous 50-year-old survivor of serious physical, emotional, sexual abuse, and neglect. She slept with a shotgun near her bed. She had previously been terrorized by her husband for years. He locked her in a room where she was held prisoner and he would tie her up and threaten to cut off her breasts. The floor was covered with newspapers, as that is where Cynthia had to relieve herself. I do not know the details of how she escaped from this horrible plight, but she did, and her husband was finally put in prison. She was still fearful of his release one day and hence she kept the shotgun close to her as she slept.

Growing up, Cynthia's mother was a sex worker and throughout childhood Cynthia was left by her mother to stay/sleep in cheap hotel lobbies behind furniture, a fake plant, or anywhere, while her mother was working upstairs. At 5 years old, this was terrifying for little Cynthia, and this was her lot in life.

When I met her, she had three grown children and she came into our agency because her youngest, Dan, had recently died in an accident. I never experienced this type of grief before. I sat with this dear mother for several sessions while she simply cried and shook before she could even speak of her aching heart which was hurting from pure, unadulterated grief. Nothing helped. No interventions here, no cognitive restructuring or reframing. Dan was dead and he was not coming back. I traveled alongside her while she told me of going to a fortune teller to see if she could find out where Dan was. She told me of a presence she felt in her room one night. I asked her what her feelings were at that moment. She said she was not afraid, as she thought it was her sweet son. She said she would go through the funeral again just to see his face.

We discussed her going to a grief group and she went once. She said she did not return there because her son's name was too precious for her to share with anyone at that time.

I learned much from Cynthia as she mentioned subject matter new to me. For example, Cynthia shared that she would sleepwalk and go to the kitchen and find her favorite candy bar and would discover the wrappers on the counter the following morning. Now specialists out there who may be reading this might say, "Sleep eating! Of course!" But I had never heard of this before. This is when I used my absolute best active listening skills, and Cynthia and I explored feelings and thoughts about why she might do this. Food nurtures, and a favorite candy bar is a decadent treat for anyone. Cynthia needed a way to survive just as she did in the hotel lobbies at night. Sleep walking provided a wonderful opportunity to sneak a treat to nurture herself when no one else would do it.

We never came to fixed conclusions about fortune tellers, feeling the presence of her son in her room, and eating candy during her sleepwalking excursions. I just explored, validated, clarified, and affirmed that life is not fully understood. The scope of experiences in the world around us cannot be placed in a specific category and fully explained.

When my dad died, I was with my son who was a year and a half old when his papa passed away. Jon was in his highchair in the kitchen and the door was open. Jon looked in the direction of the door and said clearly, "Papa!" I saw nothing, but I know Jon did. It was something that could not be proven or denied as happening. This was not in my belief system at all and did not have to be. It was comforting. That was the extent of that. When Jon was born, my dad used to come by early in the morning just to get a glimpse of him. He would have coffee and sit with his cup waiting for Jon to wake up. When he would awake, my dad would visit for a short minute and off, he would go. He just wanted to see him.

As I worked with Cynthia, I was amazed at what she went through and how remarkable she was to be able to sit in front of me as a resilient survivor of so many terrible experiences. I was also saddened that I could not sit with the five-year old in the lobby and allow her to sleep while I watched over her through the night. I could not comfort the little girl to let her know that I cared. I was in her life 50 years later and just marveled that she was there, allowing me to hear her heart. I grieve for the countless children whose story is like hers, as they are still out there.

The Children. Part of my training requirement included five hundred child/family hours. I did child hours at the agency and the rest at two elementary schools. I love working with children as they are so very transparent. They say exactly what is on their minds, unlike adults with whom therapy is like peeling an onion—layer after layer until they feel safe and know they can trust the therapist not to harm them.

Children say, "My mom never plays with me. I do not think she loves me." "The thing I hate about my parents' divorce is that we are never all together under one roof."

Statements like that seem like an easy fix: play with your children; arrange to have everyone present at a child's birthday. It is never that simple as children are often overlooked when parents' own bitterness is at stake or unforgiveness is in play when wronged. So, they bring the child to a therapist to fix them up. There is no judgment here. I have always told parents that parenting is the most difficult job on the planet. One size does not fit all. It is difficult at every stage, and it takes wisdom, grace, patience, earnest effort, and love.

At a school where I worked, we offered counseling because a young African American boy was killed in the process of his bike being stolen by a Latino individual in the neighborhood. This area was only five blocks, with three blocks being occupied by Latinos and the two blocks adjacent occupied by African Americans. It was common knowledge at the school that the person who was arrested for this homicide was an underage juvenile male who was not the perpetrator. The youngster took the "fall." It was believed that being underage, the authorities would go easier on him. The neighborhood school is a unique environment as everyone seems to know everyone's business. Honest, industrious people were parent volunteers, and all knew who killed this child. I was told as much, but no one ever broke the silence as to who it was.

Marlon. There was Marlon who lived on one of the African American blocks. He was a tiny third grader who always wore his hoodie up covering his head and eyes as if he were hiding—which he was. His world was a dangerous place to be, and he needed constant protection.

I was on the playground during recess and Marlon came running up to me and jumped into my chest full force as if I would be able to scoop him up and hold him. After knocking the breath out of me, he said, "Do you want to race to the library?" I thought, "It is interesting how this little boy, so full of life, views me. He thinks I can catch him in my arms and then try to outrun him to the library!" Marlon taught me that it was okay to be who I was. He saw me as someone safe to be with, trustworthy, and being what he needed in that moment. I did not have to be extraordinary. He saw me as someone who was there for him.

The day came when Marlon had to say goodbye. "We are moving back to Los Angeles. There they fight with bats and things; here they want to kill you with guns." What an ugly reality this eight-year-old child had to face. He was moving to where, at that time, in the nineties, it was "safer."

There are so many like Marlon, who at age eight should be running on the streets with his friends, getting into little kid mischief, throwing baseballs, and occasionally breaking a neighbor's window. Not so for him. Just going to the corner store was dangerous as the neighborhood store was guarded by the gangsters in the area and Marlon's family was not welcome there because of the color of their skin.

Juan. A domestic violence household is a terrifying place for anyone, especially a child. In addition, surrounded by community violence there is almost no place for a child to feel safe. Such was the case of Juan and his family who lived on the Latino block, with his mother who was 25 years old. She had a ten-year-old daughter, Juan who was nine, his brother who was six and a baby sister. His father was out of the home because of domestic violence, and it was an open Department of Child and Family Services case.

Juan was a handsome child with soft brown curls, hazel eyes, a quiet demeanor, and an awful life. He was intelligent and very observant. Because he was poor, he wore whatever clothes he had and came out of class one day telling me that the kids were making fun of his shorts because they were "girls" shorts. As we walked to the treatment room, I could have "explored his feelings" about how it felt when he was laughed at by the other children, then "validate" him, and problem solve around how he could manage those feelings going forward. Instead, I just told him the truth: they were a Hawaiian print and I assured him he looked fine and that men wore those as well. Not very "therapeutic," but in looking at this young boy, the "mother" in me came out as the "therapist" was angry and tired. I was also just so sad, so troubled that in addition to everything else he had to deal with in his world, he was also bullied. Like countless other children, Juan was not responsible for any of his life's circumstances, but he had to deal with the results.

I had a saying for Juan which was "Where there is smoke, there is Juan." He never did anything wrong on the playground, but he was always there, taking in everything when there was trouble brewing. One day there was a shooting on the next street where he lived, and a gang member was killed. He told me about walking over to see the crime scene with the chalk outline of where the body was on the sidewalk for days with stains of blood. This was part of his norm.

In another session, Juan came in with a frightening story about how his school bus was stopped by gangsters while commuting to school. He was agitated and described the bus driver who tried to defend the bus full of children. He was so upset. I had not heard of anything like this that day on the news and I knew that what Juan was talking about was a result of something changing in his world for the worse. The themes of his story were intense violence, fear, and defenselessness.

Juan told me that after his father was gone, the neighbor became his mother's boyfriend and would come to spend the night with her. When that happened, Juan and his siblings would all have to sleep in the living room. Four children. They knew full well what was going on in the bedroom, but they were kids and had no voice. What could they say when mom and the neighbor spent the night where they normally slept? Nothing. They just found their area of the living room and tried to sleep as best they could. What was in this child's future?

As was my usual practice, I checked in with Juan's teacher to see how he was doing in class. His teacher was the only Mexican American male on the faculty. It was near Father's Day and his teacher pulled out a Father's Day card to show me, given to him by Juan. I can only imagine that when Juan would see this tall, handsome man that he might have wondered what it would be like to have him as his dad. How does a 9-year-old boy conclude that he will go to the store to get a card for his teacher on Father's Day?

There are cards for teachers I know, but this was one for a father. He did not think it was inappropriate or that others might make fun of him; he just expressed to this teacher his feelings about him. Looking at that card broke my heart and when his teacher showed it to me his eyes were full of sadness. The card was not just a card. It told a tragic story of a fourth grader, longing for another kind of life.

Juan needed a miracle, and it never came. Years later, I heard he was in prison. At age 16, he was in the back seat of a car used in a drive-by shooting. There were four people outside the house, and none was hurt. All the people who were in the car were charged with four counts of attempted murder. Juan was not the shooter, but again, "Where there was smoke, there was Juan." I learned that Juan spent three years in prison for that crime and was released only to be convicted of homicide when he was 22 years old. Although there are certainly exceptions, this boy had his life all mapped out. He was born to a young mother who was overwhelmed, and to an angry, violent father who beat his mother. He lived on a street where survival was the only objective. Eventually, prison was the destination.

Looking back at this child, I wonder what else I could have done for him. I grieve for his family and am saddened that our system can only do so much, and that amount may never cover what is needed. Remembering Juan, he was not overtly angry or aggressive. He was never in a fight or disrespectful to anyone. He just looked at his options in life and fit in where he found a place, with others just like himself.

Angel. A fifth grader, Angel, whose mother had a drug addiction, lived with his grandmother. His mom came to the playground one day and I met her. She had missing teeth, blotchy skin and was very bloated. She was also only twenty-eight. During session, Angel would tell me that when his mother would come to visit, she took the couch where he slept and would pee on it during the night. This was difficult for Angel. Where can a child talk about the mother he wished he had, and the truth about his real mother, who wet his bed? Angel could say this in therapy with me.

Angel simply told his story. I do not ever recall having to prompt this child with "open-ended questions" or to use interventions to find out how he felt. He just told me in a matter-of-fact manner because it was not a deep-down secret; it was his existence which he lived every single day.

Angel walked with a swagger as if he had the world figured out. He intimidated other children as he would try to shove a sock down their mouth while on the playground. He was imitating a wrestler he followed on TV during that time. I know this sounds terrible and it is, but it was everyday life on the yard at school. I never saw Angel running. He walked slowly as if knowing everyone would just wait for him to show up or not. It did not matter.

Once he had a terrible cold and I asked when he was going to get it checked by a doctor. He said, "Believe me, you are the only one who cares." Angel never missed school. He would rather be sick at school than at home. I have never thought of school as a pleasant place to escape my problems, but it is a haven for many children.

Angel's grandmother did her best. She would buy him music to listen to and it was full of foul language, but these were the groups he wanted to hear. I asked him to bring some music videos with him to session so that we could watch them together, and he did. We discussed the songs and what he thought of what was being said. I asked if he would consider doing those things and why or why not, and what the songs meant to him overall. Back in the day, I learned to follow the client's process, follow the client's lead, and meet them where they were. If I did that, I found that I did not need to dig at all for information. Most of the time, I was led right to where the session needed to go, where the client would feel safe to be vulnerable and share their heart. This can only be done with genuineness and authenticity. These are things that a therapist will not and cannot fake.

I was so proud of Angel when he finally graduated from fifth grade. I saw him in line, ready to walk into the auditorium and I brought him a small stuffed dog, named Sarge. Sarge came with a little sign that said, "I will protect you."

His family was there, all in full force. His mother, her boyfriend, their daughter, and his grandmother. I told Angel I saw his family and he said, "Yeah." His family was in disarray and causing a commotion as they waited for the ceremony to begin. His little sister broke free at one point and was running all over the auditorium full of onlookers with her dad chasing her. But they were his family. I have discovered that family is family. They claim you as their own. You are connected somewhere. They show up, not always so pretty, but they are there. It was far from ideal, but Angel belonged to the people who claimed him. "Yes, Angel is with us."

Baby Girl. Baby Girl was a kindergartner who was already living in an established gang family. She came to see me because she had taken a toothbrush from a classmate, as toothbrushes were being given to all the children to promote dental hygiene. Although this was not the best way to get a toothbrush, she may have just wanted an extra one to give a sibling. Who knows? Or she just took it because she could.

Baby Girl was never well-kept, and she had no feelings around her alleged theft. She told me of her life, that they lived in vacant houses around town, and when the social workers would come by the house, all the kids would leave through an open bedroom window. She was rarely under the supervision of an adult, and that is why they had to run from the social worker. They would get in trouble if the social worker found the children alone. She was five years old.

Meeting Baby Girl's mother revealed a female in her thirties, covered with tattoos, looking tired and worn. She told me that her own father ruled the family from Folsom. It became apparent that her life was part of a generational process passed down through the years. What mode of therapy could challenge this mom to want to make different choices in her life? This is all she knew and at this point, what could be done to change the course of her existence and that of her children? Rock-solid family dynamics were in place and would continue for a long time.

Treating a child without parental involvement is challenging. When working with children in school, they must return to the same house that they left in the morning. They return to the abandoned homes, the sofas with pee on them, the front room to sleep in while mom is with the neighbor and with the routine of jumping out of the window when the social worker makes a visit. Therapists do their best, hoping that the little client will internalize something from the therapeutic relationship that will help them as they grow.

Briana. Briana had brown chestnut hair, braided into one thick braid down her back. She was seeing me because she was born with a life-threatening medical condition. Her mom wanted to have her seen as a support for her. Briana was an "A" student who stopped therapy once because she did not want to fall behind in her studies. She returned as she was preparing for another major medical procedure.

When she asked to come back, she told her mom it was because she wanted to play with me. My time with children was play therapy, as this is how children communicate. Others, when they are older, talk more, but with most children it is usually a combination of both. When we spoke about her upcoming surgery, it was minimal. She told me that she asked her doctor what type of sutures he would be using, and she would tell me when an upcoming test was scheduled. Other than that, she did not speak about it – she just played like other kids for an hour so that she could focus on something else other than death.

Briana was planning to go on a road trip with her family to the mountains when it snowed in the winter. She was looking forward to playing in the snow, but by the time there was snow, she was too sick to make the trip.

Each day at school, she and her friend would go to help pass out the snack for kindergarten classes. Soon because of her condition, she would just go to the office to sit and eat her snack as she was no longer strong enough to be the special helper of the kindergartners.

Often, I would be in the schoolyard, and I would see Briana leave her classroom and walk straight to the office without looking to the right or left, without greeting anyone. She was serious, rarely smiling. Observing her one day I thought, "Who can relate to what this child is carrying on her shoulders?" No one. Her life was different than others and she was very aware of it all.

The day came for Briana to enter the hospital for her scheduled surgery. Concurrently, my mother became ill and was going through tests. My mom was 83 years old and was in pain and the doctors were not sure of what was wrong. I was going between my mother – at the end of her life's journey—to the hospital where Briana was struggling for a chance to live her life. I could not believe that this was happening at the same time.

My mother was my sounding board, the one who would ground me, the rock who supported my siblings and me through the challenges of adult life. Because my dad died 25 years earlier, it was my mom that was the center of the wheel in our lives. My mother went to the eighth grade in school. Her education, however, went beyond the classroom walls, and even though her children were all college graduates, no one could ever outshine Mom.

My dear mother died one Tuesday morning and three weeks later Briana also passed from this life. The entire school mourned the loss of this sweet child. She was the student every teacher wished they had. I mourned them both: two of the most inspiring Mexican females I have ever known. Mom and Briana. Vicenta and Briana.

Merry. Merry was a kindergartner whose mother was terminally ill. She was a quiet child with a short blonde bob. She was referred for support. Merry would draw pictures, using art as her vehicle for sharing her heart.

I am not an art therapist, but simple projective interventions, like art, storytelling, sand trays, produce information as to what one is feeling, and it is often just under the surface of one's consciousness. One day Merry drew a water scene, sand, two chairs on the shore, and no people. In the distance was a grove of trees with footprints going into the trees. As she told me about her picture, I asked about the footprints and she responded, "So that they will find me." When I heard that, there was no interpretation needed. Merry felt lost in a forest. No people around, just the hope that she would be found. She was right in the middle of her mother's illness and dying; her father's grief and her own; and at five years old, not able to make meaning of it all. She was hoping that she would be found as she left her little footprints in the sand.

I know Merry's parents were working hard to prepare Merry for her mother's impending death. They were videotaping while making cookies together and creating memory books with letters and stories about their relationship. I am quite sure Merry enjoyed this time with her mom, but this also served as a dual purpose of Merry having these precious memories to cherish after her mom died. Amidst this, Merry still was missing something about her "present." She missed her parents.

I do not know how to fix this, as serious illness has a way of controlling homes and families. The memorabilia would be used to comfort Merry when she was older, remembering her mother. But what can be done at age five, as life is playing out in front of children? Parents can acknowledge the chaos, validate how things have changed and why, and grieve with each other. During the process they can let the child know that both parents are holding them closely physically and, in their hearts, even though it may look different. There is no simple answer.

When I first started my counseling journey, people would often make the statement, "Staying in the moment." I heard that many times and thought of it as a cliché, something that was a part of fluff psychology and never knew what it meant until this career demanded that I practice this concept. As a therapist, I have learned to stay present with my client or whoever is sitting with me, staying focused and in the moment because life is made up of moments. The client is sharing their "moments" with me. Just merely glancing off, looking at the clock, wondering what to fix for dinner will tell a client I am not interested in them. Merry helped me understand how vital "moments" are. They make up our days, our present, when we are living.

Harlan. Harlan was an 8-year-old who was living with his aunt. His mother severely abused him while he was in her care. This was all done in secret, behind closed doors. Harlan was full of anxiety and that is why his aunt brought him in for treatment. He would bite his nails, often making them bleed.

Harlan loved the sand tray. It was filled with various creatures, horses, tigers, cows, dogs, birds, dinosaurs, sheep, etc., all of which he would use to play out his history of abuse. One day the animals were all picking on one of the others in the tray. The various creatures would swoop down, taking turns biting and tormenting the little victim. As he played this out, I asked, "Where are his friends? Can someone come to help him?" Harlan answered, "No one knows."

One day Harlan came in and sat at our play table, put his head down and slumped that entire session not saying a word. I just sat with him as it was clear he was not going to speak at all. Our sessions were 50 minutes and that is how he wanted to use his time. So, we sat and sat. He never moved and neither did I. I just observed this little fellow express his fatigue, his sadness, his helplessness, and his frustration with that day all through his body language. He seemed to say, "I am so upset I do not want to sit upright in this chair. I will use this table to rest upon. I am too tired to even speak so do not try to make me say anything. I do not want to share my feelings; I am telling you how I feel by ignoring you. This is the best I can do right now."

This is the only time Harlan did this and I just let it play out naturally. As he left my office, his grandfather who brought him to session told me that he had a fight with his close friend at school. My office was a safe place for Harlan, a place to think and sort things out. He felt he could do whatever he wanted to do in his safe place, and he did.

Months into treatment, I received a call from his aunt, and she was so excited. She called me to let me know that for the first time, she had to trim his nails. Harlan had stopped biting his fingernails. Harlan bit his nails because he was full of anxiety and fear. As these feelings lessened, he relaxed and did not exhibit this behavior any longer. His aunt and I were ecstatic.

Kaylee. Kaylee was a biracial fourth grader who lived with her maternal grandparents as her mother was severely depressed and was not "attached" to this child. I remember getting the referral and going to her classroom to pick her up for our first session. The teacher told me that she and a classmate had gone to the office on an errand and that they would be back shortly. After a few minutes of waiting, two little girls came walking up to the classroom. They were both lovely. One of them was striking with large brown eyes, long eyelashes, and brown hair. When I saw her, I thought, "This cannot be the child. What mother cannot attach to this little girl? I am already attached!" But it was her, Kaylee. The child whose mother was too depressed to show her expressions of love.

Kaylee's brother was two years older, and he attended the same school. He lived with his mom. As she lived with her grandparents Kaylee told me of fishing trips that her uncle would go on and come to bring them fish on Friday nights. She would get permission to wait up as her grandma would fry the fish, which she loved to eat.

Kaylee had adapted and demonstrated how important extended family is: grandparents, aunts, uncles, and all the in-laws and "out-laws." Kaylee had her needs met, and even though she missed living with her mother and brother, she and her grandparents made it work. She told me that her grandmother made her sandwiches just from the white part of the boiled egg as she did not like the yokes. Grandma made sure that the little sandwich Kaylee brought for lunch was perfectly made for Kaylee. She was being cared for, nurtured, and loved. I believe Kaylee would carry these little "love stories" of the late-night fish fry's, the egg-white sandwiches with her through life. Nothing fancy, nothing expensive, remarkably simple, cherished memories of daily living.

Mario. Mario was a selective mute. He spoke at home with family but not at school or in front of strangers. This generally stems from anxiety, family dynamics and other variables. Without getting too technical or deep (as I am not an authority on this condition) I think Mario would consider himself a shy child.

Many of us feel we are shy, although this can be somewhat of an anathema to those who seemingly know us to be otherwise. When we find ourselves out of our comfort zone, we evaluate our surroundings and measure what we say. This is normal. Some people are always the life of the party, and when they enter the room there is the expectation that they will liven things up as soon as their first witty comment is made. Then there are other individuals who choose to be on the periphery of all the action. There are introverts and extroverts. Mario was an introvert.

Mario was a child in a new country with everything foreign to him. He was not comfortable with the language as he and his family were mono-lingual Spanish. I think that on the first day of school, he may not have been able to respond as appropriately as he wished. So, he did not respond. Or, from the start he chose not to speak for any host of reasons.

As time wore on, Mario became known as the "non-speaker." When you gain a reputation for something, it is difficult to break free from that. For a child, it would be a challenge to know when to jump in and start talking even if you want to. If you are shy, speaking would call too much attention to yourself, so staying quiet is the best and only option. When the teacher calls on you in class to make you speak, a power struggle develops as the child knows the teacher wants him to speak. In Mario's world, I do not know how many choices he had or how much control he had over coming to this country and leaving extended family and friends behind. Not speaking gave him some power. "If I don't talk, I won't be called on, and if I am called on, I will just be silent." He wins.

I do not know if this was the case, but a funny thing happened on the day that I first met Mario and his family. I had to go to his home to do the intake paperwork and received a call that my interpreter had to go to the doctor for an emergency. Mario had no phone so no one could call and cancel, and the only choice was to make the home visit. I recall driving to his home trying to figure out how to tell this family in Spanish that I had no interpreter and somehow, I had to do an intake. I left all my knowledge of Spanish in high school decades ago with my inadequate teacher, Coach Smith.

The family met me in the driveway, several little faces looking at me along with Mario, all surrounding their young mother. I explained as well as I could that we had several pages of an intake to do and that with their limited English and my dreadful minimal Spanish we could get through it.

Mom invited me in, and the family all sat around me on the floor. And so we began, first with Mario's birthdate. Me, in Spanish, "Enero, Febrero," and thankfully Mario was born in February and so I wrote that down. Next was the day, "Uno, dos, tres" and as my pronunciation was so "gringo" Mario himself spoke up and clearly, said, "25!" His response was firm and loud. A miracle happened! He spoke. In front of a total stranger. No prompting needed, just someone butchering his first language until he could no longer bear to hear it.

I drove back to the office and related to my colleagues how I just cured a selective mute! Of course, I had not, and I did sit with Mario in sessions for several months, wherein he did not do any speaking. I would talk and process what we were doing until he would look at me with his deep brown eyes clearly imploring me not to speak. So, I would say, "Do you want me to stop talking?" And he would nod his head "yes." In retrospect, this little guy may have just wanted peace and quiet in this busy world full of noise and drama.

Katrina. Individuals need to be validated by others in their struggles. Such was the case with 13-year-old Katrina who was depressed and had passive suicidal ideations. She was in therapy for a while previously, and new to me as a client. She was in Special Education classes at school, and for many children this can be a tough situation to be in. She began speaking about how it was for her as her friends knew which classes were Special Education and the classes were emptied at the same time when the bell rang. All the kids knew that she came out of *those* classrooms. As she described this to me, I said to her "Katrina, that must be hard for you to do that every day." She responded emphatically, "THANK YOU, PRISCILLA! Everyone tells me that I am just as good as everyone else, and that this is temporary, and I will not have to be in Special Ed forever." She was tired of people trying to "turn her frown upside down." The frown was real, and she needed that seen and understood. As she brought this out in the open, we had a fair playing field. We could discuss her thoughts and feelings and explore interventions on ways to negotiate life.

We all have challenges, and we are different. As an individual plays the hand in the life they have been given, they can begin to see where they may have a lack, according to the societal measure in which they find themselves. They can acknowledge it and set about to improve in that area if they choose and have the opportunity. They can also discover other gifts that they have that they can honor and showcase. We have seen examples of this repeatedly. Individuals who are "overcomers" are in this category because they persevere, are encouraged, and receive love from their supporters. It may only be one supporter, or they may have to be their own support. But somehow, they make it happen.

Chapter Five

Moving On

After being at the first agency where I worked for 15 years, there was a shift in the organization, and it was time for me to leave. It had become a toxic environment and unfortunately this place where I was allowed to grow and develop since graduate school, became an unsafe place to be. I thought this was going to be my home until retirement, but alas, it was not.

As the day approached for me to depart, I realized I had lost a gold hoop earring. I found it later in the break room, on a shelf, and it was bent and crooked as it had been stepped on. I thought, "That earring looks like me." Bent and broken.

I remember walking out by myself, around 7 pm, telling the new receptionist it was my last day. He is the one that came around from behind his desk to wish me well and to give me a hug. The bosses were angry that I was leaving, and this was my exit--a young man, I barely knew gave me my send-off. It was fine with me. A least it was genuine.

I had no job but was not really looking for another position as I had no idea where to start. I was sitting in my den one day and a former colleague called me as she was seeking a professional reference for a therapist I had supervised. After discussing the individual, she said, "I am looking to hire a supervisor so if you know of anyone, let me know." I responded, "You may be speaking to one." She clarified that her office and the position were in South Los Angeles.

I did not know where that was, so she explained it to me, and we set up a time to meet. I remember driving there, going north on one freeway, and then catching another to take me east. I never went this way before, and the scenery was vastly different from where I worked previously. No ocean breeze and upscale neighborhoods were nearby, rather there was the crowded congestion of the inner city with random pit bull sightings.

As I drove, I arrived at my destination, which was an older, small office building wherein the agency lay and did business. I gained entrance by being buzzed in and my colleague was locked in her office reviewing clients' files.

On the wall outside her office was the map of the area where the building was located, and it colorfully designated the various gangs in the neighborhood. When I studied it, I was determining where not to drive, however at closer inspection, the building was in the middle of gangland; and since the work was in the community, in homes, there was no escaping one gang or the other.

Where the gangs were located was a moot point. As I learned to negotiate my surroundings when driving through the city, I always stuck to the main streets. If there was a detour, I could easily get lost in the small streets and did this a few times.

Once I noticed a black van at an intersection. It turned in front of me and the van's side door was open, revealing several individuals inside. A man was holding his hand out to the oncoming cars along with my car signaling for us to stop. When I saw the open door I thought, "Oh my, that's unsafe!" Then I realized it was an unmarked police vehicle that held officers ready to jump out of the van at the nearby housing project. But I digress.

My colleague opened her door and after greeting each other, she told me a little about the position. There was no interview per se as we knew each other and just had to settle the finer details of salary, hours, and of course, if I wanted to work there.

I went through the hiring process and began my role as a clinical supervisor. I provided both individual and group supervision with teams of individuals, as this agency offered Wrap-around (WRAP) and Full-Service Partnership (FSP) which are intensive services. By this time, I had been supervising for seven years. I was also hired to deliver direct treatment to clients at this large and growing non-profit agency.

The cases were challenging as our clients suffered from multiple traumas, living amidst community violence. As I heard about the presenting issues, my heart was troubled by the severity. Unfortunately, they were all like this. There were no easy cases; no one just needing a self-esteem boost.

As mentioned earlier, in my previous position, I was one of a few ethnic minorities, but here in South Los Angeles our teams were reflective of our population, coming from all zip codes and countries throughout the world. They were from various levels of society. Our staff included individuals from Mexico, Guatemala, Peru, Ecuador, Venezuela, Columbia, and India all with rich histories and much to contribute to clients we served.

The company was contracted by the Department of Mental Health (DMH) and at the time I was hired, we began to use treatment methods that research had shown were proven to work. This was what was being funded by DMH. General therapy (using various theories) was out the window as everyone was trained in the treatment models. Clinicians had additional supervision to make sure there was adherence to the prescribed course of treatment, and it was time limited.

As I began to work with the clinicians, I noticed that they were right out of college and were immediately trained in a trauma treatment model, as this was our agency's focus. I, myself, was trained with everyone else in working with trauma and in addition, I was trained to lead children and parent groups. We taught social skills to the children, shaping their behavior, and offered parenting for their caregivers.

Any manner of treatment needs to be couched in solid, basic clinical skills. New college graduates often lacked this. The model guided the treatment, and there were specific steps to be followed. A seasoned clinician would know how to integrate the model into their sessions, but others could not do this. They would become confused as to how to start with "Part One" of the treatment and still meet the client where they were at in that moment with "unconditional positive regard" (Rogers, 1961.) How to do this was part of the training I provided in supervision with my team members--the basics of the therapeutic process.

CHAPTER SIX

GROUPS

As I was trained, I began facilitating groups in 2009 and did this until 2016. On Wednesday, I would work in the child group and on Thursday, I would work in the parent group. There were two facilitators per group, so I usually worked with an associate.

At first, the parent groups were challenging because our parents were often court-ordered to attend. As a mother myself, I knew how it was to answer for negative behaviors of my own children when the teacher would call. Parents may feel that it is their fault or that schools think that they are terrible parents. Others feel guilty or resentful of the "system" in place asking them to attend parenting. Therefore, every first group session was usually quiet with skeptical individuals wondering how this group could help them turn things around to the satisfaction of all concerned.

This is where I came face to face with more of the people whose stories I am sharing in this book. The following group members were from separate groups. During the year, we would have two groups, one in spring and fall, with weekly sessions for 20 weeks.

Our groups began at 4:30 pm and went until 6 pm. At the end, parents could earn a certificate which would enable them to present the parenting group as proof they fulfilled a court requirement.

I worked with the English-speaking group and a colleague led the Spanish-speaking group. Since our population was mostly Hispanics and African Americans, the English group was made up of African American moms, grandmas, dads, and grandpas. We also would have foster caregivers in the group who were there because their foster child was referred for some negative behavior and was being seen in the children's group.

Silver. One of the young mothers in the group was Silver, a young gang member trying to raise her child amidst the complexities of life. She was lots of fun, always contributing to the group. She loved the blue eyes of my co-facilitator, a 40-something gorgeous male, who for some, I felt was the main reason they attended the group so faithfully. I thought, "Maybe I'd be looking forward to Thursdays too so that I could sit and look at him for an hour and a half." Who knows? Might be a respite, especially after a difficult week living life.

One evening Silver came in with a bruised face and she told me a man attacked her with a cane. Of course, I went to my "concerned place" as she had been hospitalized as a result. She said, "Don't worry Priscilla, it has been taken care of." I kept going as I often do not know when to cease and desist, and she just repeated herself that "it" was taken care of. Although I was only 20 minutes from home, this area of the city took care of their business in their own way, living the best they could while using the resources available to them. Drop it, Priscilla, "it" was "taken care of."

Gemma. Learning the language and culture of this community brought new revelations. Gemma was in the group for her son and at the beginning of group one session she said that she had been "knocked" down resulting in a limp she had that evening. I thought she tripped on something and so I pursued with, "How did that happen?" A wonderful foster mom was sitting next to Gemma and said to me, "She got knocked down!" Although that is exactly what

Gemma said, when Charity repeated it, that clarified matters at once: someone knocked Gemma down. I do not know why this was so unbelievable, but it was. It was amazing to me that this young woman would still have the energy to come to the group, after being physically hurt by someone.

Gemma reported in another group session that she had tried an intervention with her son, trying to reach the goal of having him make his bed. She said it did not work, and she proceeded to relate to the group why it did not work: she had asked him to do two things rather than just one, as we were changing one behavior at a time. While living with domestic violence Gemma was still determined and ready to be effective in her parenting for the sake and love of her son. Incredible.

As you drive through South Los Angeles, you will see lots of churches. Some are large but most are small, and there are many people of various faiths who came through our doors. I mentioned Charity earlier, and she would come to our groups whenever she had a child being referred who was under her care. These children were fortunate to have her foster them. In Los Angeles County, there are tens of thousands of children in the system who have been abused and/or neglected and need a loving home. Our children have been abandoned and it is up to the county system to make up for the lack in our society.

We often take it for granted that we can sleep in a clean bed at night and quietly drift off. Not so for many of our most vulnerable and helpless populations. Children go to bed frightened, emotionally empty, and hungry. They are trying to drown out the fighting and punching going on in the next room, putting their pillows over their heads to muffle the terrifying sounds.

When a child comes from a domestic violence household, many times we are told by the parent that the child was in the other room, outside, never hearing any of the fighting. My follow-up question to that would not be spoken aloud, but I would have liked to ask: "Who was caring for your children when you were beating the life out of each other?" And of course, the children saw domestic violence most of the time—if not directly, then the aftermath. In many instances, the cycle they become accustomed to is repeated throughout their lives.

Charity. Charity had two of our clients in her foster home during one group cycle. She said that at bedtime, when she would walk past the boys' room, they were kneeling in prayer with one leading the other. I have sat with that visual for years and have never forgotten it. Two children taking care of each other. Praying together. There are caregivers like Charity, and it is a wonderful thing. Unfortunately, this is not always the case. Too often, children are removed from terrible homes and deposited in households where they are re-victimized. The vicious cycle continues until someone like Charity opens her heart and her home to these little ones.

Vincent. Vincent was the group favorite. He was 59 years old, an ex-convict who obtained full custody of his 8-year-old daughter, Diamond as her mom lost her parental rights. Diamond was the result of a one-night stand. Vincent came to parenting classes as his daughter was having some behavioral issues.

He was transparent and that is why he was loved by the group. Unexpectedly and completely out of context, he said to a young woman across the room wearing large gold earrings, "Years ago, I would be looking at those earrings wondering what they were worth." He was relating his old self to us, so we would know exactly who he was before, but not now.

He would go on to say, "I wake up in the morning thanking God, and then go to Diamond's room to look to see if she is breathing and thank God again." He loved the group, and we loved him back. He told us about two months before the group would end that he asked Diamond, "What are we going to do on Thursday nights from 4:30 to 6 when the group is over?" Vincent was already counting the days to when the group ended, as the support meant a lot to him and his daughter.

One day Diamond's individual therapist told me that Diamond had been hit on her arm by Vincent and it left a bruise. We had to call it in to make a report. When these things happen, we first speak with the parents, when it is possible and appropriate. We let them know that a report must be made and remind them that at the beginning of therapy, we made full disclosures about child abuse laws and that we are mandated reporters. When making the report itself, we also let the Department of Children and Family Services (DCFS) know that the client is in treatment with us and faithfully attends and takes part, if that is the case. Vincent understood; the call was made and the social worker from DCFS went out to investigate.

I knew before the group the following Thursday that the report was made and DCFS had gone out. I fully expected the "fallout" from the report, and I was just so impressed with the group as they managed the entire thing. My co-facilitator and I just saw the powerful dynamic this group had developed. The group was safe and could tolerate whatever its members wanted to say. They could validate, affirm and problem solve and come to their own conclusions. Their feelings were not hurt, there was room for questions, clarifications were made, and self-disclosures were heard. No one was judged, rather cared for in one of the most skilled ways I have ever seen. They spoke from experience and did not need the professionals to insert themselves. It was extraordinary.

Vincent spoke and let the members know what happened. He said that when the social worker arrived, she asked to speak alone with Diamond after speaking with him. He said, "Of course."

His anger came out, and so did the anger of the group, whose doors at home revolved with people coming through at will, to examine them and their families. DCFS can go into a home at any time they wish depending upon the severity of the accusation and sometimes with the police in attendance. This was not the case with Vincent, as the infraction was one that just needed a visit at that point.

The response of the group was a chorus, all in sync. After sharing their hearts, the discussion continued and at some point, turned the corner, realizing that yes, things like this can happen. They were at the mercy of the authorities and since they were, how could they go forward? This was life. This is life. Choices must be made.

Laura. Laura was quiet and was the only Hispanic in our group of African Americans. She preferred the English-speaking group so that she could practice her English. Her daughter had issues at school revolving around language, ironically enough, as she would call classmates the "B" word but use the Spanish translation. Laura learned quickly that her daughter was mimicking her own use of that word which she said at home all the time.

At the end of the group during our last meeting, Laura, who looked up to Vincent, I believe as a father figure, had purchased two neckties. One was for Vincent and another one for a young father in our group. These groups were organic and grew and developed a closeness that could not be forced. It was a natural cohesiveness that resulted from consistent meeting with others, hearing their stories, and sharing their own, all without judgment. No one in our groups "cast stones" rather they knew that each one had a road to walk and the best way to negotiate that road was to have someone who knew what it was like to be in their shoes. Empathy.

As Laura gave each man their necktie, it was such a joy for me to see her and them work together helping with the correct way to tie the knot. Humanity, one on one. No committees, no laws on how to treat someone, just being human. It was a simple demonstration of kindness that was a spontaneous gift of a moment in life.

Scarlet. Scarlet, a 50-year-old great-aunt, had gained custody of three great-grandnieces under the age of ten, all with special needs. She wanted to keep them "out of the system." Otherwise, the girls would be sent to strange foster homes. Scarlet stepped up in a big way, like many extended family members who do the same thing. It can be a great sacrifice, with difficulties faced along the way, but also can deliver great rewards.

As this group assembled for the first time, Scarlet stated emphatically: "I do not hug, and I do not play." She let me know she was there but not to expect anything--setting firm boundaries. Scarlet was always dressed up with her hair and nails freshly done.

One of the topics we covered in the group was how to play with our children. Often the parents wanted to start with how to discipline their child or the consequences they could administer for wrongdoings. Our programs began with how to play with one's children. At times, parents were resistant and felt silly sitting and doing floor time, playing with blocks or cars together with the facilitators and each other. I really enjoy role-playing, as whenever I have role-played the part of a client, and I start to say the client's words, I begin to feel empathy for the client whose words I am speaking. That is simply my experience.

One session, my co-facilitator was playing the child in role-play and the parent was supposed to be commenting on what the child was doing. If the child were putting the car in a certain place the parent would say, "Oh, I see you have put the blue car in front of the driveway," pointing out the color if it is a small child just learning colors, and where it was placed. As the play progressed, the mother became harsh in her comments. She said things like, "Why did you put it there and not here? You cannot put the car there as it is in front of a driveway!" In free play, a child can do and put the car anywhere they want. They do not know the laws but rather are moving and making things happen in their play world. They have some control. The objective of play is just that: "play." Having fun, laughing, enjoying being able to break the "rules" can be therapeutic. Also, they can have input when they are usually powerless and without a voice.

My co-facilitator was doing her best but was clearly getting overwhelmed with this parent's commentary. Role-play would last long enough to emphasize what was being taught. After the role-play, I checked in with both participants and asked them how it was for them to do this demonstration. I do not recall what the parent said, and often they just would respond that "It was okay," but my co-facilitator said, "I felt like crying."

My co-facilitator, a recent graduate, was 26 years old at the time. When she played the role even though it was not real, she may have been triggered by her own critical parent recollections or was just troubled that a child would have to go through this with their parent. Clearly, role-play evokes emotions as it did here: fear, rejection, powerlessness, anger, and sadness. It has been a tool that I have always used.

Scarlet had to sit through weeks of this. Then one session, she shared in our check-in that one of her nieces hugged her. I responded, "What did you do?" Scarlet said, "I hugged her back!" as she began to laugh and do her happy dance with her legs which she did periodically to show her joy. That was a huge milestone for Scarlet as folks do not hug for many reasons. It may mean that touch is not welcome, that it has been painful, or physical affection was left out of their upbringing, etc. It was the first hug for Scarlet, and she was delighted to share it with her group members.

Jack. When a new group started, I never looked at their histories, as I prefer to hear the story from the parents without any preconceived ideas, and therefore I would not know who was in the group. As I opened the session the first night, there was a tall, athletically built young male who came. I was delivering my spiel as I normally did, giving the parents an overview of what to expect, attendance requirements, etc. As I addressed the room, I would glance at everyone to make sure all felt included and began to build rapport. Each time I looked at this young person, he was staring at me with what seemed to be an unusually hard look and I began to wonder why.

I was already a grandma, and I am small and non-threatening in my appearance. I always tried to be welcoming and convey honesty and trust. The hard looks kept coming however, and so at the end of the group I made it a point to go to sit beside him and find out a little about what he was feeling or thinking. His name was Jack and as I sat, he said, "Is this group legit?" asking if this group would fulfill the court-ordered parenting class he needed to gain custody of his daughter. I told him "Yes" that it would meet the requirement.

Jack committed to the group and shared in the process. As I got to know him better, I spoke to him after session one night and mentioned college to him. He responded, "Oh, I already have my AA. I got that in prison." I suggested he continue to his bachelor's degree. Jack said he would. I do not know if he did, but I was grateful that I met him, as despite great barriers he found a way to make things work and could be a role model for his little one. Yes, an individual can find a way through a setback, get on the road again and make one better choice at a time. On the way, you can inspire others to do the same if they wish.

Mindy. Mindy was a sex worker who had substance use problems and by the time we met, she had given birth to eight children, none of which she was ever allowed to hold. All the children were detained at birth and were placed in foster homes. She had gained custody of two of the children and they came to the group for various behavioral concerns. Mindy came and sat quietly in the corner of the room with her legs crossed and arms folded tightly across her chest.

I cannot even imagine the courage it took for this young woman to show up. She was there for her children and for weeks, she just observed. When we would do demonstrations on how to play with the children, I could hear Mindy say softly to herself, "Oh, I see, that is how it is done." She had never seen or heard anything like this before. One night when our group was small, she began to speak saying, "You know, my mom comes by and loves on my kids, but she never did that to me." I gently asked her if she thought she could mention that to her mother and she replied, "Oh no! She is my mom!" That showed to me the respect she had for her mother and that relationship. She would never call her mother out for something lacking from her childhood. She had longed for affection her entire life but simply did without it.

The group was problem-solving one night and we were brainstorming ways about how to get the children into class on time, as the gates at the school closed at 8 a.m. By this time, Mindy was an integral part of the group and she said that she would get the children up and dressed and they would walk to school. The children would be in line outside the gates and Mindy would go to the tamale vendor nearby to get the children tamales and a drink for breakfast which they would eat while in line. I was so impressed with Mindy's solution and praised her over and over for her ingenuity! I have used Mindy as an example over the years, as to how to make things work through the challenges of life, when there does not seem to be a way.

One night Mindy was missing from the group, and someone reported that she was arrested. She had a fistfight with a neighbor and spent a couple of nights in jail. When she returned to the next session, she looked wonderful! I cannot say why, but at one point I thought maybe she had a little rest and recuperation—who knows? Perhaps she saw some of her old friends. I am not making light of this; I am simply saying that there is an entire world out there that we do not know anything about, but life continues without skipping a beat. People just make do.

Patricia. Patricia was going through a program in which she was learning how to cook, and the program would help her to find a job. She announced to the group, "I got a job!" We were thrilled for her as she began to tell us more and I was wondering if she was cooking in a restaurant or what. As it turns out she was making cookies at home, for a marijuana clinic down the street. When I heard that I thought, "Oh no!" and then started going down my "assessment list." I set aside time to speak with Patricia alone to address my concerns as we never want to put a group member on the spot or to shame them in any way. Where are the children when she is baking? Where are the supplies kept? What safety precautions is she taking? Does the social worker know that she is doing this? Patricia would bake when the children were at school; the supplies were kept at another place and the social worker knew and approved the job.

Patricia shared with the group again another evening about a tragic event in her past. She told the story of having a little baby girl who was born with multiple congenital birth defects. She spoke of how her daughter was going through surgery after surgery and that she was suffering tremendously. And then, she continued relating her story. "My family thought that I killed her; I did not, but I prayed that she would die. She died in my arms in a shelter." I was sitting on the arm of a sofa, as our group was large. Her story saddened the entire group so deeply and I almost started crying. I had to steady myself so that I would not fall off the sofa's arm. I was completely stunned that Patricia went through all of this in a shelter, with complete strangers. She was estranged from her family and alone. I was so touched by her courage, honesty, and transparency by telling this group about being accused of killing her baby. Patricia was torn and guilty, but her prayers were answered, as her little girl was no longer suffering. I cannot know this mother's heart. I just know my heart. Mothers carry loads that they cannot always share, and Patricia trusted this group so much that she revealed her soul to them that Thursday night long ago.

The reader may wonder how these stories all came out during the parenting group, as this was not group therapy per se. We managed to cover all our material, but material cannot be divorced from the individuals who will be using it or from their lives. People would recall how they were disciplined or how they were not played with during their childhood and tell the group how it was for them. When someone would talk about child abuse laws, a parent would say, "Where was DCFS when my dad was knocking the heck out of me?" Our groups flowed naturally as the members joined together and even formed relationships outside the group.

Beatrice. Because these were mostly all DCFS cases, parents had already been advised about hitting their children. Beatrice related how her children would tell her that she could not hit them, as this was against the law and that they would just call the social worker if she did. This mom felt she had no choice but to discipline them by having them kneel on the floor holding their arms up straight over their heads as this was how her parents punished her. Individuals usually use the same discipline methods as they had used on them when they were children. As Beatrice spoke, another mother was sitting a few chairs away and began to cry softly. When I checked in with her, she spoke of how her dad used to do that to her and how painful it was for her to endure. We all listened and although no one said anything else, this young mother who brought it up was given a bit of insight into what her children were feeling.

As our groups were cross-cultural, there were differences in ways to correct a child. Group leaders had to be sensitive to this and reiterate what our laws were and then leave it to the group to come to their own conclusions, and they usually did as in this case.

A professor of mine used an example of a pot of soup. One may make the recipe repeatedly, never deviating from it one iota. Then one day, the cook may decide to add a bit more salt, an extra bay leaf or a pinch of nutmeg. The soup is automatically different. People who eat the soup may not know about the alterations and not recognize that the soup is different. It tastes the same, but it is not the same soup. In a family system when something changes, eventually the entire system must make an adjustment to that change, or try to maintain the equilibrium, bringing back the "old recipe" -- to the original way things were done.

Ebony. An illustration of "the soup" was given by a young mother, Ebony, who was in the parenting group and her five-year-old son was in the children's social skills group. Ebony said that they were at a family birthday party and her son had brought along one of his toys. During the event, her son came to her and said his cousin took the toy and would not let him play with it. Ebony, who was a bit of a "fighter" herself said, "Go and get it back from him!" Previously this is exactly what the child would have done, as that is how he learned by the age of five how matters like this were settled. However, he told his mom, "We are going to leave in a while anyway; I will just get it then."

Mom was so amazed that her little son problem solved this all on his own without resorting to his normal way of reacting, which was to become aggressive. She knew as she told the group this story that she had to adjust her response to her child having a cooler head. She needed to use other problem-solving strategies rather than physically fighting over everything.

People often resort to hitting and punching, as that is the only thing that they may know. There is no other way for them to get their point across or their needs met. It is important when we see changes in our children for the better that we notice those with a "good going" a simple "high five" as these types of reinforcers are always great to have. Parents often remark only on the negative because when they see positive behavior, they may feel that the child should know automatically how to respond in an acceptable way. That is not always the case for a child who only sees disagreements in the home quickly escalating to yelling and then physical fighting. Children learn many ways and when something is played out in front of them, they learn very quickly. Especially when they see it daily.

Victor. Something changed in Victor's world, a 9-year-old in a social group my colleague Lorraine and I facilitated. He came in because he was being bullied at school. His grandmother was in parenting. Victor would always raise his hand when a question was being asked in the group, and when called upon he would say, "Uh, I don't know." This could happen ten times during a group—truly.

Lorraine and I had a simple curriculum, played games with the children, and even used a beach ball to play our form of "volleyball" in the not-so-big treatment room. We had fun.

As our group was nearing completion, we asked each child how they were doing. Victor said, "I am not bullied anymore." Lorraine and I were ecstatic. I asked what changed. What happened? His answer was the same, "Uh, I don't know." As I was wishing he could point to something he learned in group so we could use it again successfully with other children, I thought, "No, this is very cool." Victor could not attribute his not being bullied to an outside intervention or source. He just knew he could walk down the halls at school and not be teased. Was it his acceptance in our group by the other children which impacted him? Was it his grandmother responding to him differently because of what she had learned? Was he walking taller and owning his space? I will never know, and it is okay that Victor did not know either. He just knew he was no longer a target. The soup was different.

I recall sitting in my practicum one night and I raised my hand and asked my professor, "Why does therapy work?" This was something I often thought of, as this career was unknown to me. I had no idea why sitting speaking with someone would help a person therapeutically. Her answer without hesitation was, "love." Love? That was news to me! In therapy, the client often speaks about not being loved etc., but my professor sounded as if the "love" would be part of the therapeutic process. There are extremely strict boundaries, legally and ethically around "romantic love" and the word "love" itself. It can be easily misinterpreted by a client who is depressed and lonely, or anyone for that matter. Therefore, "love" was not a word I ever used in my relationship with my clients.

From what my professor said, I understood that there must be an investment in the client with whom one is working. Humanity in the therapist should be recognizable. Once in group supervision, our supervisor mentioned that she would be gone the next week as she was leaving on vacation. Because we were a polite group, we showed interest in what she said and asked where she was going. No one thought of packing a bag to go with her; it was just a question that was a natural follow-up to what she just said. To our amazement, she stammered and would not say where she was going. Boundaries should be strict and according to the law, and a therapist would quickly assess how much of a disclosure is warranted given the circumstance and who is asking the question. This supervisor was bound by the book and did supervision according to a handbook. I felt that she, herself, was missing from the equation.

So back to "love." Reflecting on what my professor said, she meant that warmth and genuine caring about the client is needed in the relationship. A cold and distant therapist cannot make the human connection needed in the therapeutic alliance. Disliking a client is not effective either and can be damaging.

Betty. As a new ignorant therapist, I used to believe that I could work with anyone until I met Betty who was the mother of five children, all under 10 years old. I was working with her on parenting and self-care and supporting her kindergartner who was not doing well in school. Her little one had trouble doing his homework and so I suggested that she could sit with him while he did his work. "What? Sit with him? Then I would have to do that with all my kids!"

As a mother myself, I knew my children benefited from me being nearby while they did their homework, mostly as a grounding presence. They could also just ask a question if needed. My feelings about this client needed to be checked as I found myself struggling when I had to go into the session with her. Working with Betty taught me that if you cannot stand someone, you are the wrong therapist for them. (This may seem obvious but sometimes a therapist may want to try to make the relationship work to keep the client for various reasons, even though it is not a good match.) As I was new, still a trainee, my active listening skills were not as good as I wished and with her, I was exasperated most of the time. I had no empathy for this person. When she resisted my suggestion of sitting with her child I could have said, "It sounds like it is overwhelming to be a single parent of five children and having to be the one the kids always rely on for help. It must be exhausting. How do you do it?"

When supervising my team, I hear some who sound just like I felt with this client. I ask, "Do you like this person?" Sometimes the answer is "Yes," and then we talk about what it is about them that makes them likable. We talk about what it is that triggers them as well. Then we problem-solve around how to approach the barriers with the client. This is usually done by bringing it up with the client in an appropriate way so that the relationship itself can be examined.

Sometimes the answer is "No, I don't." Then I ask if they think that the client can tell. Because clients can usually tell if they are disliked, especially wounded ones who are on guard against anything that resembles rejection. It is then that I work with the supervisee to see if they can discover why the client is so disagreeable and how they got that way. We must realize that many individuals in the client's life feel about the client just like the therapist does. This will hopefully bring the therapist into a more empathetic place and just like the soup, change the recipe in the room. It happened rarely, but if the issue could not be resolved, referring the client out was and is the only clinically appropriate choice.

CONCLUSION-HOPE AND ENCOURAGEMENT

I recently asked someone why they chose to be a therapist, and they responded, "To give people hope." I have asked many people this question, but this is the only time I received this answer. The heart of what I have learned as I have remembered and reflected upon the lives of the people shared here is that hopelessness is a killer of the human spirit.

My father was a pastor of a small Christian congregation when I was growing up. We had "youth nights" and during these times of fellowship, a teen was asked to give a talk, like a short sermonette. I was asked on a few occasions and I would always ask my dad about what I should say. He replied, "Something that will encourage the people." Encouragement, hope –letting people know that despite life's, at times, devastating challenges, it can be done. My faith led me to this career, and I believe that as I worked with others, God has been my strength and has given me the much-needed wisdom I needed to go through each day.

Of all the clients I have treated, Juan and Baby Girl were the two that I have grieved the most. All the rest have had an ex-convict waking up in the morning being grateful to have a child brought into their life at the most inopportune time; others have had a warm and comforting foster parent welcoming them home after school with a snack and good meal; many have had a great aunt take them in and experience the journey that led to an unexpected hug. They had someone in their lives who would humble themselves and attend a parenting class so that they could learn to make better choices for their children, whom they loved.

To the grandparents who support with the fish fries, to the ex-sex worker who provides her children with a nutritious breakfast waiting in line for school, to the countless teachers, neighborhood mamas and grandpas who provide a haven for throw-away kids, you have made such a difference. I honor you for making the sacrifice for one child or a hundred who have come looking for someone to care for them.

To the many therapists I have worked with who go into this career with the thought of helping someone find their way, keep doing what you do, and thank you. When it seems hopeless, remember that the recipe for the soup changes with every smile you give and someday it will blossom, hopefully into something beautiful.

Becoming a therapist has been a calling and ministry for me. I have reaped so much more than I have sown. What a privilege to see people, truly see them even though we drive the freeways. I am thankful for the off-ramps which have brought me closer to moments of real living and have expanded my life in such an abundant way.

REFERENCES

Perls, Frederick, Hefferline, Ralph, Goodman, Paul. *Gestalt Therapy*, 1951

Raposo, Joe. "One of These Things" (Is Not Like the Others,1968)

Rogers, Carl. *On Becoming a Person*, 1961